To "The Girls"

Claire Elizabeth

Abigail Jane

Rinnah Kathryn

Kayley Grace

Psalm 127:3

If this is your first encounter with *A Taste of Columbus*, you may be surprised to learn that we are 22 years old. A lot has changed since 1978 when we published our first cookbook, both with our city and its restaurants, and with our family.

When we published our first book, my husband and I were parents of three small children. Since we have always thoroughly tested every recipe in our books, those early tasting sessions were unique, to say the least. For our children, macaroni and cheese always won out over veal piccata or calamari.

Today our family has grown to include another son, spouses and grandchildren - fourteen in all. My daughter-in-law Katy has joined me in producing this book, and I now have four granddaughters to offer their candid opinions on the dishes we test. Macaroni and cheese still wins out for the younger set, but we trust that the more sophisticated eaters in your household will appreciate the chefs' favorites included here.

Once again, as she has for the last two volumes, my eighty-two-year-old mother-in-law has produced the wonderful pen-and-ink drawings that capture the flavor and charm of our city. She has included a self portrait on page 4, and all four of her great granddaughters can be

A Taste of Columbus
VOLUME V

Favorite House Recipes
from over thirty of
Central Ohio's Leading Restaurants

Beth Chilcoat and Katy Chilcoat

Artwork by Mildred Chilcoat.

Typesetting by Jennifer Fenner.

We gratefully acknowledge the help of the following:

Charles Arn

Mary Jane Arn

Connie Berry

Andy Chilcoat

David Chilcoat

Ed and Barbie Chilcoat

Jeff Chilcoat

Mike and Kimie Chilcoat

Andy Fenner

Carol Malone

Nathan and Jenny Shaw

Becky Skinner

found on pages 21 and 33. Also, guess who the chefs are on the back cover!

We gratefully extend a heartfelt thank you to all the chefs who have shared their delightful recipe secrets through the years, and especially to those represented in this current volume. Volume V of A Taste of Columbus is a virtual "Who's Who" of Columbus' best chefs.

We hope that you will have fun experimenting with the recipes in our book. Possibly you will sample new dishes and attempt new processes that will deliver delicious results. We know that you will encounter dishes that will delight you with their simplicity, eye-catching appeal and mouth-watering flavor.

Happy Cooking!

Beth Chilcoat

Katy Chilcoat

Alana's
Barcelona
Biddie's Coach House
Brookside Golf and Country Club
Cameron's
Cap City Diner
Columbus Brewing Company
Dick Clark's American Bandstand Grill
Engine House No. 5
Firdous
First Watch
Katzinger's
La Chatelaine
Latin Rooster
Martini Italian Bistro
Michael Dominic's Steak and Seafood
Mitchell's Steak House
Morgan House
Polaris Grill
R.J. Snappers
Red Door Tavern
Refectory
River Club
Sapporo Wind
Seven Stars at The Worthington Inn
Shaw's Inn
Siam Restaurant
Spagio
Starliner Diner
Taj Palace
Top Steak House
Trattoria Roma

Contents

APPETIZERS

M. Chilcoat

Victorian Village

Mitchell's Steak House
CALAMARI
Recipe of Chef David Dovell

1/4	cup pickle relish
1 1/2	tablespoons rinsed and chopped capers
1	tablespoon minced shallots
1	tablespoon minced fresh Italian parsley
1/2	teaspoon salt
	Pinch ground black pepper
1/2	cup mayonnaise
1 1/2	teaspoons Dijon mustard
1/4	teaspoon Tabasco sauce
1/2	cup flour
1 1/2	teaspoons Creole (Cajun) spice*
7	ounces calamari
1	tablespoon butter
1	teaspoon minced garlic
1	teaspoon chopped fresh parsley
1	tablespoon seeded and julienned pepperoncini peppers
1	tablespoon seeded and julienned cherry peppers
	Salt and pepper
	Lemon wedges

In bowl, combine first 9 ingredients to make rémoulade sauce for calamari. Set aside.

In bowl, combine flour and Creole spice. Toss calamari with flour mixture until fully coated. Deep-fry calamari until golden.

In small pan, melt butter. Add garlic and parsley. Add both peppers and sauté briefly. Toss with calamari.

Season with salt and pepper. Serve with lemon wedges and rémoulade sauce.

Makes 1 large serving.

* This product is available at Big Bear.

The Fountain at Easton Town Center

Polaris Grill

GARLIC BREAD
WITH GORGONZOLA SAUCE

Recipe of Chef Tom A. Callaghan

1/2	cup water
1/2	teaspoon chicken bouillon
	Pinch salt
	Pinch black pepper
	Pinch ground white pepper
2 1/4	teaspoons minced garlic
2	tablespoons butter
2	tablespoons flour
1	cup heavy cream
2	ounces imported, crumbled Gorgonzola cheese
1	tablespoon grated Reggiano Parmesan cheese
	Dough for 2 pizza crusts
2	tablespoons oil
1/2	teaspoon basil
	Pinch minced garlic
	Grated Reggiano Parmesan cheese
	Fresh Italian parsley, shredded

Place water, bouillon, salt, black pepper, white pepper and garlic in small pot. Bring just to boil, making sure bouillon is fully dissolved. Remove from heat. Set aside.

In another pot over medium heat, cook butter and flour

together until thick. Slowly add bouillon liquid, mixing constantly until smooth. Reduce heat to low. Stir constantly for 4 to 6 minutes until mixture forms a thick paste. Slowly add cream, stirring constantly, until smooth. Simmer 3 to 5 minutes or until thick and creamy. Fold in Gorgonzola and Parmesan cheese. Set aside.

Roll out 2 pizza crusts and place on hearth stones (or pizza pans). Bake at 475° for 8 to 10 minutes or until crust is puffy and golden brown. Remove from oven.

In small bowl, stir together oil, basil and garlic. Brush over crusts. Top crusts with Gorgonzola sauce. Garnish with desired amount of Parmesan cheese and Italian parsley. Place under broiler until golden brown. Serve immediately.

Makes 2 pizzas.

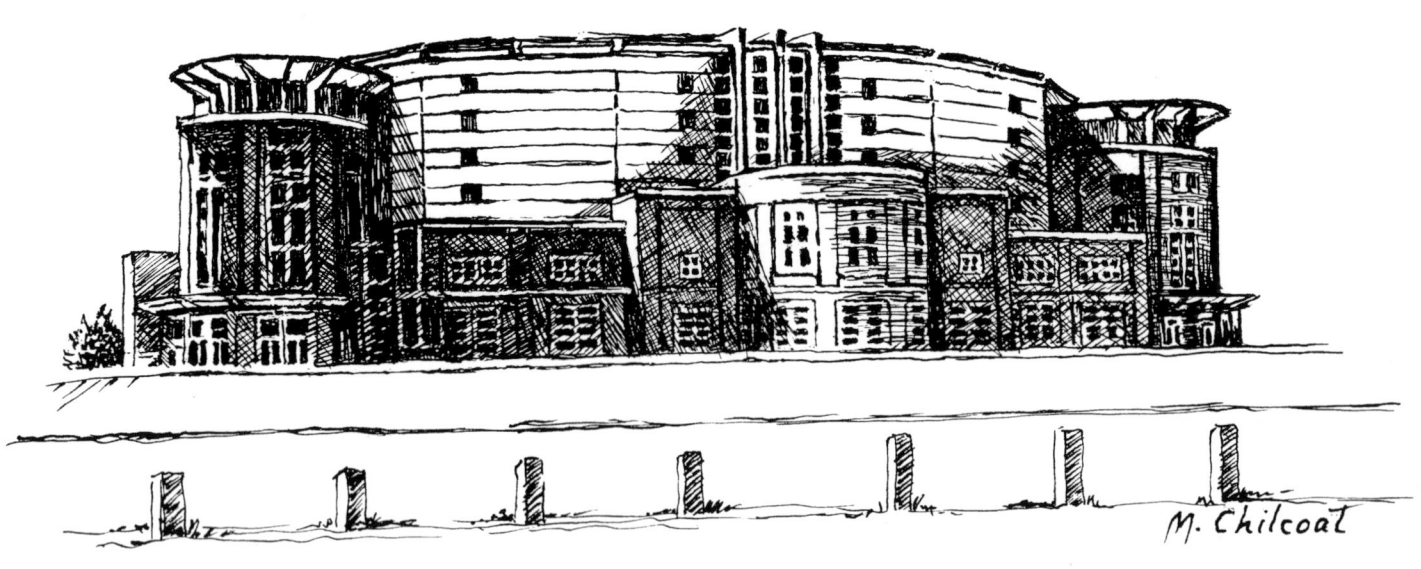

The Schottenstein Center

Barcelona
GRILLED PINEAPPLE AVOCADO SALSA
Recipe of Chef Paul Yow

1	pineapple
6	ripe avocados
1/2	cup diced red onion
1/2	cup diced red pepper
1/2	bunch green onions, diced
1 1/2	tablespoons minced garlic
2	tablespoons lime juice
1 1/2	tablespoons Tabasco sauce
2	tablespoons white balsamic vinegar
1/4	cup olive oil
	Salt and pepper

Peel, quarter and core pineapple. Grill quarters. Dice grilled pineapple into 1/4-inch pieces. Set aside.

Peel and dice avocados. Set aside.

Place diced pineapple, red onion, red pepper and green onion into large bowl. Mix together remaining ingredients. Pour over pineapple mixture. Add diced avocado and mix carefully so as to avoid mashing avocado.

Serve with tortilla chips or with fish or chicken.

Makes approximately 1 quart.

Morgan House
Honey-Lime Fruit Sauce
Recipe of Chef Chris Meadows

1/3	cup honey
1/4	cup Key lime juice
1	egg, slightly beaten
1/4	cup brown sugar
	Pinch salt
1	tablespoon rum (optional)
1	teaspoon cinnamon
1/2	teaspoon nutmeg
1	cup sour cream

In small saucepan over low heat, combine honey, lime juice, egg, brown sugar and salt. Cook and stir until thickened, about 10 to 15 minutes. Do not boil. Remove from heat and stir in rum and spices. Place in refrigerator until completely cool. Once chilled, fold in sour cream and blend well. Refrigerate at least one hour before serving. Serve over fruit salad or as dip for fresh fruit.

Makes approximately 2 cups.

Refectory
Hot Cheese Puffs
Recipe of Chef Richard Blondin

1 cup water
1/2 cup unsalted butter
1/4 teaspoon salt
1 cup flour
5 eggs, room temperature
1/2 cup grated imported Gruyère cheese

Preheat oven to 350°. Line cookie sheet with waxed or parchment paper.

In heavy saucepan, bring water, butter and salt to boil. Add flour and stir vigorously until smooth. Continue to cook over medium heat for 5 minutes, stirring constantly.

Transfer to mixing bowl. Using mixer, beat in eggs one at a time. Add cheese and beat for an additional minute.

Drop by rounded tablespoons onto cookie sheet. Bake until puffed and golden brown, 20 to 22 minutes.

Makes approximately 2 dozen.

Spagio

PIZZA APPETIZERS

Recipe of Chef Hubert Seifert

2   garlic cloves

4   ounces sun-dried tomatoes packed in oil (Drain tomatoes, but reserve 2 tablespoons oil.)

1   teaspoon chopped fresh basil

2   tablespoons grated Parmesan cheese

1   loaf sourdough bread

2   tablespoons olive oil

     Parmesan cheese

To make pesto, purée garlic cloves in food processor. Add sun-dried tomatoes and 2 tablespoons reserved oil. Add basil and cheese. Purée again.

Preheat oven to 375°.

Slice bread to desired thickness and toast on baking sheet for 5 minutes.

In small bowl, combine 2 tablespoons olive oil and sun-dried tomato pesto. Mix well.

Spread on toasted slices of bread and sprinkle extra Parmesan cheese on top.

Bake for an additional 5 minutes or until cheese has melted.

Makes 6 to 8 servings.

Sapporo Wind
SAPPORO CALIFORNIA ROLL
Recipe of Chef Tadayoshi Horoiwa

2   cups short- or medium-grain Japanese rice*

1/4   cup rice vinegar*
1   tablespoon sugar
1/2   teaspoon salt

2-3   large sheets of dried seaweed (nori)*
1   softened, peeled avocado, cut into thin strips
4   ounces crabsticks, cut into strips

1/3   cup soy sauce
1/2   cup mirin (Japanese rice wine)*

6   ounces barbecued eel*
Roasted sesame seeds

1   ounce wasabi powder,*
   mixed with enough water to make thick paste
Pickled ginger slices*
Soy sauce

Wash rice and drain. Place in rice cooker or saucepan and cook according to package directions. Set aside.

Mix together rice vinegar, sugar and salt. Pour on rice and gently mix together with flat spatula without crushing rice kernels. Allow rice to cool to room temperature.

Cut each nori sheet in half. Place nori sheet flat onto sheet of plastic wrap. Coat hands with water and small amount of

11

vinegar to make handling of rice easier. Spread about one cup of rice over each halved nori sheet. Pick up nori and rice, leaving plastic wrap on counter and flip over. Nori is now on top. Place avocado strips and crabsticks on top of the middle of each nori sheet. Gently roll into cylinder shape and flatten top for eel piece. Remove plastic wrap and set sushi roll aside. Repeat for other 3 to 5 sushi rolls.

To make eel sauce, mix together soy sauce and mirin. Set aside.

Broil eel for 3 minutes and brush on eel sauce. Slice eel in half lengthwise and slice width in half (if using whole barbecued eel). Match size of eel to size of sushi roll and place eel on top of each sushi roll. Sprinkle with sesame seeds. Cut each sushi roll into 6 pieces.

Serve immediately with wasabi paste, ginger slices and soy sauce.

Makes 4 to 5 servings.

* This product is available at Japanese markets.

Dick Clark's American Bandstand Grill
SASSY DIP
Recipe of Chef Israel Santiago

2	cups Alfredo sauce
1/4	pound Asiago cheese, grated
1/2	teaspoon minced garlic
1	teaspoon pepper
1/4	teaspoon Tabasco sauce
1/4	teaspoon marjoram
1/4	teaspoon crushed red pepper flakes
1/2	cup cooked and drained chopped spinach
1/4	pound $^{150}/_{200}$-count cooked shrimp
2	tablespoons grated Parmesan cheese
1	Roma tomato, diced

Heat Alfredo sauce in pan to simmer. Add cheese and seasonings. Mix well. Add spinach and heat through. Remove from heat and stir in shrimp. Place in small casserole dish. Sprinkle with Parmesan cheese and lightly brown under broiler. Remove from oven and sprinkle with tomatoes. Serve with tortilla chips.

Makes 6 to 8 servings.

The Top Steak House
SCALLOPS WITH
ROASTED RED PEPPER SAUCE
Recipe of Chef Ken Yee

2	red peppers
1	teaspoon salt
1	teaspoon pepper
1	tablespoon minced garlic
1	teaspoon red pepper flakes
2	tablespoons basil
3/4	cup olive oil
1	tablespoon balsamic vinegar
1	pound large sea scallops
	Salt and pepper
2	tablespoons oil

On baking sheet, roast red peppers at 450°, turning often until blackened, approximately 10 to 15 minutes. Cool slightly. Remove seeds and core. Peel.

In blender or food processor, blend together red peppers, salt, pepper, garlic, pepper flakes and basil leaves. Slowly add olive oil and vinegar. Blend until smooth. Set aside.

Season scallops with salt and pepper to taste.

In heavy skillet, pan-fry scallops in oil until desired doneness.

Serve red pepper sauce over scallops.

Makes 4 to 5 appetizer-sized servings.

Soups

TO HONOR THE IMMIGRANTS
THE STRENGTH OF OUR NATION
A GIFT TO THE CITY OF COLUMBUS
FROM
THE UNITED ITALIAN AMERICANS
FOR 1992

M.Chilcoat

Battelle Park

Polaris Grill
ALPHABET NOODLE SOUP
Recipe of Chef Tom A. Callaghan

2	cups diced onion
1	cup diced celery
3/4	cup diced carrots
1/2	teaspoon minced garlic
1 1/2	teaspoons olive oil
1 1/2	quarts chicken broth
1/2	teaspoon chopped fresh thyme
1	pound cooked chicken, cubed
6	ounces ABC pasta*
	Salt and pepper

In large pot, sauté onion, celery, carrots and garlic in olive oil until carrots are soft. Add chicken broth, thyme and chicken. Bring to boil. Add pasta and cook until done. Add water if needed. Salt and pepper to taste.

Makes approximately 2 quarts.

* This product is available at Big Bear.

Brookside Golf and Country Club
ASIAN CHICKEN NOODLE SOUP
Recipe of Chef Jay Yardley

1/2	chicken
2	quarts chicken broth
1/2	cup julienned shiitake mushrooms
1/4	cup julienned carrots
1/4	cup julienned leeks
1	tablespoon sesame oil
1 1/2	tablespoons chopped fresh parsley
1/4	cup soy sauce
1	tablespoon honey
	Salt and pepper
6	ounces Chinese wonton wrappers

Roast chicken for 45 minutes at 375° or until done. Allow to cool; remove meat and set aside. Save bones.

Heat broth with bones; allow to simmer 20 minutes.

In large pot, sauté mushrooms, carrots and leeks in sesame oil for ten minutes. Add parsley, soy sauce and honey. Strain broth into vegetables. Discard bones. Add water as needed. Add meat and season to taste. Heat through.

Julienne wonton wrappers. Fry in olive oil or peanut oil until crisp.

Garnish soup with fried wonton noodles.

Makes 5 to 6 servings.

Polaris Grill
CRAB CORN CHOWDER
Recipe of Chef Tom A. Callaghan

1/4 cup butter
1/2 cup flour

2 tablespoons clarified butter
1 medium onion, diced
2-3 potatoes, peeled and diced
1 16-ounce can corn, drained
6 cups water
2 tablespoons chicken bouillon
1 16-ounce can cream-style corn

2 1/2 cups heavy cream
1 bay leaf
1/4 teaspoon white pepper
3 drops Tabasco sauce
1/4 teaspoon cayenne pepper
1/4 teaspoon salt
12 ounces crabmeat

In small pan, melt butter. Add flour to make roux. Cook over low heat for 10 minutes, stirring constantly. Set aside to cool.

Heat clarified butter in large pot. Sauté onion until translucent. Add potatoes and corn; sauté briefly. Add water, bouillon, cream-style corn and cream. Bring to boil; reduce heat and simmer for 20 minutes, stirring occasionally.

Add some chowder liquid to roux. Continue adding liquid and whisk together until roux becomes liquid. Pour it back into chowder and simmer for another 15 to 20 minutes, stirring constantly. Add seasonings.

Just before serving, remove bay leaf and add crab meat.

Makes 3 quarts.

19

Columbus Brewing Company
DUCK SAUSAGE CHOWDER
Recipe of Chef Joe Cottage

1	pound ground duck sausage*
1 1/2	cups beer
2	small potatoes, peeled and diced
4	onions, diced
2	cups shredded cabbage
2	red peppers, diced
1	sweet potato, peeled and diced
1	tablespoon olive oil
1/4	cup flour
1	quart heavy cream
1	cup chicken broth
1/2	teaspoon chopped fresh thyme
1/8	teaspoon cayenne pepper
1/2	teaspoon black pepper
1/2	teaspoon chopped fresh oregano
1	cup grated pepperjack cheese
	Salt and pepper
	Croutons
	Minced chives

In skillet, brown sausage. Pour beer over sausage and deglaze pan. Remove from heat. Set aside.

In large pot, sauté vegetables in olive oil for 15 to 20 minutes. Add sausage with beer to sautéed vegetables. Add flour and stir. Add cream, chicken broth, thyme, cayenne pepper, black pepper and oregano. Cook for 20 to 30 minutes over medium heat or until potatoes are soft. Stir in cheese. Season with salt and pepper.

Garnish with croutons and chives.

Makes 6 servings.

* Duck sausage is available at some specialty meat shops. Regular pork sausage may be substituted, but avoid overly spicy sausage as the chowder itself is spicy.

The Ohio State Fair

Barcelona

GAZPACHO
Recipe of Chef Paul Yow

1	46-ounce can tomato juice
2	cucumbers, diced
1	red pepper, diced
1	green pepper, diced
1	yellow pepper, diced
1/2	cup diced red onion
1	tablespoon minced garlic
2	tablespoons fresh lime juice
1	tablespoon Tabasco sauce
2	tablespoons balsamic vinegar
2	tablespoons extra virgin olive oil
	Salt and pepper
	Sour cream

In medium-sized bowl, combine all ingredients except sour cream. Cover and refrigerate for 24 hours.

To serve, top with sour cream.

Makes 12 servings.

A Dick Clark's American Bandstand Grill

Idaho Potato Soup

Recipe of Chef Israel Santiago

1/4	cup butter	Bacon bits
1 1/4	cups diced yellow onions	Shredded Cheddar cheese
6	tablespoons flour	Sour cream
1	quart water	Green onions, sliced
1/4	cup chicken broth	
3/4	teaspoon salt	
3/4	teaspoon pepper	
3/4	teaspoon paprika	
1/4	teaspoon basil	
1/2	teaspoon Tabasco sauce	
1	cup heavy cream	
1	cup milk	
5-6	medium potatoes, diced	

In medium saucepan on low heat, melt butter. Add onions and sauté until onions are translucent. Stir in flour and cook 4 to 5 minutes. Slowly add water and chicken broth, stirring constantly so no lumps form. Add seasonings, heavy cream and milk, stirring to combine. Add potatoes and simmer for at least 45 minutes or until potatoes are tender and soup thickens. Stir occasionally. Do not boil.

Serve topped with bacon bits, shredded cheese, sour cream and green onions.

Makes 4 to 6 servings.

LENTIL SOUP
Recipe of Chef Nasir Latif

1   yellow onion, chopped
1   tablespoon olive oil
1   cup split red lentils
6   cups water
1   tablespoon cumin
    Pinch salt
    Pinch pepper
    Juice of one lemon

5   garlic cloves, minced
1   tablespoon olive oil

In medium saucepan, sauté onion in olive oil until golden brown. Add lentils and sauté together for an additional 5 to 10 minutes. Add water. Bring to boil. Add cumin, salt, pepper and lemon juice. Reduce heat and simmer for at least 2 hours or until lentils are tender.

Right before serving, in separate pan sauté minced garlic in olive oil for 5 minutes. Add to soup and serve.

Makes 4 servings.

Michael Dominic's Steak and Seafood

NEW ENGLAND CLAM CHOWDER

Recipe of Chef Nick Hutras

3	slices bacon
1/2	cup finely chopped onion
1/4	cup finely chopped celery
1	garlic clove, minced
2	tablespoons finely shredded carrot
1	bay leaf
2	tablespoons Chablis
	Dash Tabasco sauce
2	cups chopped clams
4	cups clam juice
1	large potato, cubed
1	cup milk
1	cup heavy cream
3/4	cup butter
3/4	cup flour
3/4	cup water
	Salt and pepper

In large pot, fry bacon until crisp, being careful not to burn. Break bacon into small pieces. Add onion, celery, garlic, carrot and bay leaf. Sauté mixture until tender. Add Chablis and Tabasco sauce. Cook 1 minute.

Add clams, clam juice and potatoes. Cook for 10 minutes.

25

Remove from heat and slowly add milk and cream. Return to stove and cook for 20 minutes.

While soup is cooking, prepare roux by melting butter over low heat in medium saucepan. Stir in flour. Add water and stir until it forms a paste. Slowly add ladles of hot soup to roux while mixing thoroughly. Continue to ladle hot liquid into roux until mixture is creamy. Slowly add roux mixture back into clam chowder and mix thoroughly. Cook until desired consistency. Season with salt and pepper. Remove bay leaf before serving.

Makes 6 to 8 servings.

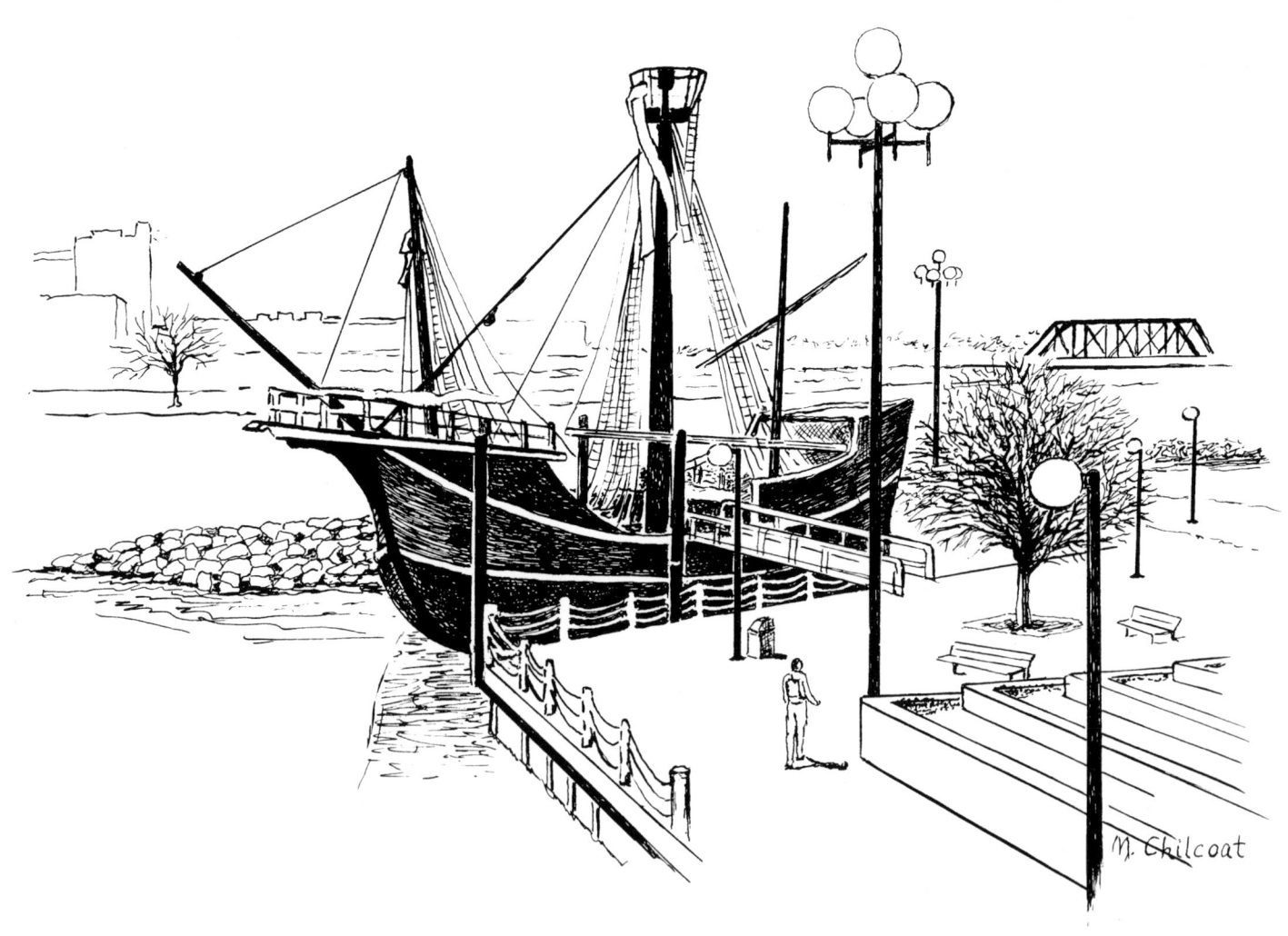

Santa Maria

Starliner Diner
ONION JALAPEÑO CHEDDAR SOUP
Recipe of Chef Jerry Burgos

1	tablespoon olive oil
1	cup minced onion
2-3	fresh jalapeños, minced
1-2	garlic cloves, minced
1	tablespoon onion powder
1	tablespoon garlic powder
2	cups whole milk
2	tablespoons heavy whipping cream
1/4	cup butter
1/4	cup flour
1/2	cup shredded Cheddar cheese
	Salt and pepper
	Diced green onions

Place olive oil in large pan. Over low heat, sauté onion, jalapeños and garlic until tender, making sure not to brown. Stir in onion powder and garlic powder. Add milk and cream. Heat just to boil. Reduce heat and simmer for 5 minutes.

To prepare roux, in separate pan melt butter. Add flour. Stir until it forms a paste. Slowly add roux mixture to soup, stirring thoroughly.

After soup thickens, remove from heat and stir in cheese. Add water as needed. Season with salt and pepper. Garnish with extra shredded Cheddar cheese and diced green onions.

Makes 4 to 6 servings.

Biddie's Coach House
PLUM SOUP
Recipe of Proprietor Mary Marsalka

3	1-pound cans of pitted plums
1 1/4	cups water
3	tablespoons sugar
1/4	teaspoon cinnamon
1/4	teaspoon white pepper
1	tablespoon plus 1 teaspoon cornstarch
1/2	cup plus 2 tablespoons dry red wine
2	tablespoons lemon juice
1	tablespoon plus 1 teaspoon grated and minced lemon peel
1/2	cup plus 2 tablespoons heavy cream
	Salt
1/4	cup sour cream
1	tablespoon raspberries

Drain plums, reserving syrup. Purée plums and pour into saucepan. Stir in syrup, water, sugar, cinnamon and white pepper. Place cornstarch in small bowl. Add small amount of plum mixture to cornstarch and stir until smooth. Add back to plum mixture. Bring to boil. Reduce heat and stir in wine, lemon juice, lemon peel and cream. Simmer 20 minutes. Salt to taste. Serve hot, or chill for 4 hours.

Blend together sour cream and raspberries. Garnish each serving of soup with dollop of sour cream and raspberry mixture.

Makes 10 servings.

Cap City Diner
ROASTED CREOLE TOMATO SOUP
Recipe of Chef Jimmy Mohammed

2 1/2	pounds Roma tomatoes, halved
1/2	teaspoon cayenne pepper
3/4	teaspoon paprika
	Pinch white pepper
	Pinch black pepper
1/2	teaspoon chopped fresh thyme
3/4	teaspoon chopped fresh basil
1/2	teaspoon chopped fresh oregano
1/2	teaspoon onion powder
1	medium onion, chopped
2	tablespoons olive oil
3	tablespoons minced garlic
1	quart chicken broth
3/4	cup heavy cream
2	tablespoons sugar
1 1/2	teaspoons salt
2	tablespoons tomato paste
2	tablespoons butter
2	tablespoons flour
2	tablespoons water

Lay tomato halves on baking sheet, cut side up. In separate bowl, mix together cayenne pepper, paprika, white pepper, black pepper, thyme, basil, oregano and onion powder. Sprinkle mixture over tomatoes. Broil tomatoes until spices are well browned. Remove from oven.

In large heavy pot, sauté onions in olive oil until soft. Add broiled tomatoes and garlic. Cook over medium heat until tomatoes are fully soft and breaking down. Add chicken broth, cream, sugar, salt and tomato paste. Simmer 20 minutes.

While soup is simmering, in small pan melt butter over low heat. Add flour and cook 2 minutes. Add water and stir until smooth. Remove from heat. Set aside.

Allow soup to cool slightly. Purée. Pour soup back into pot. Add small amount of soup to butter/flour paste and stir until smooth. Add back to soup to thicken. Strain soup for smooth texture, if desired. Heat soup and serve.

Makes 1 to $1^1/_2$ quarts.

Dublin

Engine House No. 5
TOMATO-BASIL-PARMESAN SOUP
Recipe of Chef Jeff La Pointe

1/4	cup vegetable oil
1	cup finely diced celery
1	cup finely diced onion
1	cup finely diced carrots
1	tablespoon basil
1	teaspoon oregano
1/2	bay leaf
3	cups canned tomatoes with juice, puréed in food processor
1	quart chicken broth
1/4	cup butter
1/2	cup flour
1	cup grated Parmesan cheese
2	cups half-and-half
1	teaspoon salt
1/4	teaspoon ground white pepper

Heat oil in 4-quart soup pot. Add celery, onions and carrots. Sauté for 5 minutes. Add basil, oregano and bay leaf. Add tomatoes and chicken broth. Bring soup to boil; reduce heat and simmer approximately 15 minutes or until carrots are tender.

As soup cooks, prepare roux by melting butter in saucepan, adding flour and cooking over low heat for 5 to 7 minutes.

With ladle, add small amounts of broth to roux, stirring after each addition until a smooth paste forms. Keep adding soup broth until about 4 cups have been added. Add water to soup as needed. Add roux mixture back into soup and return soup to simmer. Add cheese and whisk well. Warm half-and-half and add to soup. Stir in salt and white pepper. Simmer soup for 15 to 20 minutes, stirring occasionally. Discard bay leaf.

Makes 8 servings.

Lunches, Salads, Side Dishes

M. Chilcoat

The Columbus Symphony's Popcorn Pops

Cap City Diner
APPLE RAISIN CHUTNEY
Recipe of Chef Brian Hershey

4	Granny Smith apples, peeled and diced
2	tablespoons raisins
1/2	cup cider vinegar
1/4	cup granulated sugar
1/4	cup brown sugar
1	teaspoon minced garlic
1/4	teaspoon nutmeg
1/4	teaspoon cinnamon

In saucepan, mix together all ingredients and cook over low heat for approximately 45 minutes, adding water if needed. Stir occasionally. Mixture should appear shiny and sticky when done.

Serve with Pork Chops with Apple Glaze (page 71), Skillet Beans (page 53) and Buttermilk Mashers (page 39).

Makes 4 to 6 servings.

Shaw's Inn
Asian Sesame Cole Slaw
Recipe of Chef Denise Denman

½	large head cabbage, thinly sliced
3	cups shredded carrots
2	cups thinly sliced fresh spinach leaves, stems removed
1	cup rice vinegar
½	cup sesame oil
½	cup sugar
3	tablespoons minced fresh ginger
1½	tablespoons soy sauce
3	tablespoons roasted sesame seeds

In large bowl, combine first 3 ingredients.

In medium bowl, whisk together vinegar, oil, sugar, ginger and soy sauce until sugar dissolves.

Toss cabbage mixture with dressing. When ready to serve, sprinkle with sesame seeds.

Makes 10 to 12 servings.

Morgan House
Baked Italian Melt
Recipe of Chef Chris Meadows

6	slices sourdough bread
2/3	cup pesto sauce
1	pound sliced baked ham
1	cup banana pepper rings
12	slices Mozzarella cheese

Preheat oven to 350°.

Place bread on baking sheet. Spread pesto sauce over slices of bread. Divide ham among bread slices. Top each with hot pepper rings and two slices of cheese. Bake until cheese is melted and sandwich is heated through.

Makes 6 servings.

Seven Stars at The Worthington Inn
BASMATI RICE
Recipe of Chef Joseph M. Harris

2	cups basmati rice
6	cups water
1	tablespoon salt
2	tablespoons salad oil
2	tablespoons water
1/2	cup plus 2 tablespoons sugar
1/2	teaspoon cinnamon
1/4	teaspoon ground saffron
1/4	cup diced cranberries
1/4	cup golden raisins
3/4	cup finely julienned carrots

In large pot, combine rice, 6 cups water and salt. Bring to boil. Stir once. Reduce heat and simmer rice for 13 minutes or until al dente. Pour into colander and drain. Place rice in large baking dish. Blend in oil. Set aside.

In saucepan, combine next 6 ingredients and heat until sugar dissolves. Add carrots and cook until mixture becomes light syrup and carrots are tender. Remove from heat. Pour over rice and gently blend. Place clean cloth on top of rice to absorb moisture, keeping cloth inside rim. Cover pan with foil, making sure no part of cloth is outside of foil or pan. Bake at 350° for 25 to 30 minutes.

Makes 10 to 12 servings.

Cap City Diner
BUTTERMILK MASHERS
Recipe of Chef Brian Hershey

6   peeled Idaho potatoes
1/2   cup buttermilk
1   cup butter
2   tablespoons chopped fresh chives
    Salt and pepper

Place potatoes in pot and cover with water. Simmer until done. Drain. Heat buttermilk and butter. Mash potatoes and slowly add buttermilk/butter mixture, beating well. Season with chives, salt and pepper.

Serve with Pork Chops with Apple Glaze (page 71), Apple Raisin Chutney (page 35) and Skillet Beans (page 53).

Makes 6 to 8 servings.

Cameron's
CELERIAC MASHED POTATOES
Recipe of Chef Fred Braun

2   large stalks celery, diced
1   tablespoon oil

10   Idaho potatoes
1   cup butter
$1^1/_2 - 2$ cups milk
      Salt and pepper

Sauté celery in oil over low heat until tender, stirring occasionally. Purée. Set aside.

Peel potatoes and cook in boiling water until done, about 35 to 40 minutes. Drain potatoes and beat with mixer. Add butter. Add milk until potatoes reach desired consistency. Add celeriac purée. Mix well. Season with salt and pepper.

Serve with Walnut Encrusted Salmon (page 83) and Red Onion, Celery and Apple Compote (page 49).

Makes 10 to 12 servings.

Katzinger's
CHAMPAGNE CHICKEN SALAD
Recipe of Owner Diane Warren

1/3	cup Champagne mustard*
1 1/2	tablespoons Dijon mustard
1/2	cup plus 1 tablespoon mayonnaise
3/4	cup sour cream
5	pounds boneless chicken breasts, cooked and cut into 3/4-inch pieces
2	stalks celery, cut on bias 1/4-inch thick
1	carrot, julienned
1	tablespoon finely chopped fresh basil
1/2	pound seedless grapes, split

In large bowl, combine first 4 ingredients. Add chicken, celery, carrots and basil. Stir in grapes. Chill until ready to serve.

Makes 12 servings.

* This product is available at Katzinger's.

First Watch
Chicken Salad
Traditional House Recipe

1   pound boneless chicken breast, cooked and diced
$1/2$ cup water chestnuts
$1/2$ cup raisins
$2/3$ cup diced celery
$1/3$ cup cubed Granny Smith apples
$2/3$ cup mayonnaise

Combine all ingredients. Chill until ready to serve.

Makes 4 servings.

M. Chilcoat

German Village

Latin Rooster
ENSALADA DE LANGOSTINOS CON MANGO
Recipe of Chef Vicenta Aracen

2	cups cooked langostinos*
1	red pepper, diced
1	green pepper, diced
1/4	cup lemon or lime juice
2	teaspoons minced garlic
1	tablespoon capers
1 1/2	teaspoons Dijon mustard
1/2	cup mayonnaise
	Salt and pepper
	Romaine lettuce
	Mango slices

Toss together first 9 ingredients. Place on bed of lettuce and surround with mango.

Makes 4 servings.

* Shrimp, lobster or crab may be substituted.

Morgan House
GOLDEN HAM STACKS
Recipe of Chef Chris Meadows

8	ounces cream cheese, softened
1/2	cup butter, softened
1/2	cup grated Parmesan cheese
1	teaspoon paprika
1/2	teaspoon oregano
1/2	teaspoon garlic powder
4	English muffins
1	pound shaved baked ham
8	tomato slices

In large bowl, combine cream cheese and butter. Stir until smooth. Add Parmesan cheese, paprika, oregano and garlic powder. Mix well. Set aside.

Split English muffins into 8 muffin halves. Toast halves.

Spread 2/3 of cream cheese mixture evenly over cut surface of 8 muffin halves.

Top each half with ham and tomato slice. Top each tomato slice with dollop of remaining cream cheese mixture. Place on baking sheet and broil until golden brown.

Makes 4 servings.

Katzinger's
GREEN BEAN CARROT DILL SALAD
Recipe of Owner Diane Warren

1 1/2	pounds green beans, trimmed
2	tablespoons white wine vinegar
1	teaspoon salt
	Pinch pepper
6	tablespoons olive oil
6	carrots, julienned
1	shallot, minced
1	tablespoon dill weed

In large pot, place beans in boiling water. Boil for 30 seconds. Drain and rinse with cold water. Drain again. Set aside.

In bowl, combine vinegar, salt and pepper. Whip vigorously, while slowly adding olive oil to emulsify.

Place beans, carrots and shallot in separate bowl. Add dill. Cover with dressing. Mix well. Serve chilled.

Makes 8 to 10 servings.

*F*irdous
JERUSALEM SALAD
Recipe of Chef Nasir Latif

5   ripe tomatoes, diced
2   cucumbers, diced
2   bunches chopped fresh Italian parsley
1   bunch chopped fresh mint leaves
    Juice of 1 lemon
5   garlic cloves, minced
7   tablespoons tahini sauce*

In medium-sized bowl, combine all ingredients. Mix thoroughly. Chill for at least 1 hour. Serve as salad or as dip with pita bread.

Makes 6 to 8 servings.

*This product is available at the North Market.

Biddie's Coach House
RASPBERRY VINAIGRETTE
SALAD DRESSING
Recipe of Proprietor Mary Marsalka

1	cup vinegar
1/4	cup raspberry liqueur
6	ounces frozen raspberries, thawed
1	teaspoon Dijon mustard
2	tablespoons sugar
2	teaspoons sour cream
1	cup salad oil
	Salt and pepper

The day before serving, in medium bowl combine vinegar and raspberry liqueur. Add raspberries and soak overnight.

The next day, place raspberry mixture in blender. Add mustard, sugar and sour cream. Blend. Slowly add oil. Season with salt and pepper. Chill one hour before serving. Serve over mixed greens.

Makes approximately 1 quart dressing.

Martini Italian Bistro
RATATOUILLE
Recipe of Chef Rick Lindeboom

1/4	cup oil
2	cups diced eggplant
1	cup diced zucchini squash
1	cup diced yellow squash
1	cup diced red pepper
1	cup diced green pepper
1	cup diced red onion
1	cup diced tomato
2	tablespoons sherry vinegar
2	teaspoons minced garlic
1/4	cup butter
	Salt and pepper

In large pan, heat oil over medium heat. Add eggplant and cook until soft, about 5 minutes. Add squash and cook for 5 minutes. Add peppers and cook for 5 minutes, adding more oil if necessary. Add onion and cook for 5 minutes. Add tomato and cook until vegetables are soft. Add vinegar, garlic, butter, salt and pepper to taste.

Serve with Tuna with Chopped Herbs (page 82).

Makes 4 servings.

Cameron's
RED ONION, CELERY AND APPLE COMPOTE
Recipe of Chef Fred Braun

1 1/2	cups minced red onions
1	large unpeeled apple, diced
1 1/2	cups diced celery
1	tablespoon white vinegar
1	tablespoon sugar
1	tablespoon olive oil

Place all ingredients in saucepan over low heat until heated through. Do not overheat or compote will discolor. Cover and let stand for 10 minutes.

Serve with Walnut Encrusted Salmon (page 83) and Celeriac Mashed Potatoes (page 40).

Makes 6 servings.

Mitchell's Steak House
ROASTED CORN SALSA
Recipe of Chef David Dovell

6   ears corn, shucked and cleaned

1   red pepper, diced
1   tablespoon minced fresh cilantro
3   tablespoons rice wine vinegar
1   bunch scallions, sliced $1/8$-inch thick
    Salt and pepper

Grill corn until cooked through. Cool and cut from cob. Toss together corn and remaining ingredients.

Makes 6 servings.

Olentangy Bike Trails

The River Club
SALMON SUMMER SALAD WITH CHAMPAGNE VINAIGRETTE AND TROPICAL FRUIT RELISH
Recipe of Chef Michael Wolf

6	tablespoons Champagne vinegar*
6	tablespoons white balsamic vinegar
4	teaspoons Dijon mustard
2	teaspoons salt
1/4	teaspoon white pepper
1	cup olive oil
1	cup salad oil
1	ripe mango, peeled and diced
1	ripe papaya, peeled and diced
1/2	red pepper, diced
1/2	small Vidalia onion, diced
1/3	cup chopped fresh cilantro leaves
1/4	cup chopped fresh chives
1	tablespoon chopped fresh mint leaves
1	tablespoon white balsamic vinegar
2	tablespoons sugar
	Salt and pepper
2	tablespoons olive oil
4	5-ounce salmon fillets
	Salt and pepper
2	heads Belgian endive
2	cups Boston lettuce, bite-sized pieces

7	cups mesclun lettuce
1	cup Mandarin oranges, drained
1	cup red seedless grapes, split
1	cup diced red pepper
$1/4$	cup pine nuts, toasted

To make Champagne vinaigrette, whisk together vinegars, mustard, salt and pepper. In very slow stream, whisk in olive oil and then salad oil until emulsified. Chill.

To make tropical fruit relish, in separate bowl toss together next 9 ingredients and season with salt and pepper. Chill.

In large preheated non-stick skillet, add olive oil. Season salmon with salt and pepper. Sear for 3 minutes on a side or until desired doneness. Remove from heat.

Assemble salad by arranging endive in spoke-like pattern on 4 plates. Toss together lettuce, fruits and red pepper with desired amount of vinaigrette, and portion onto center of plates. Arrange salmon fillets on top. Add scoop of relish on plate. Top with pine nuts.

Makes 4 servings.

* This product is available at Carfagna's.

Cap City Diner
SKILLET BEANS
Recipe of Chef Brian Hershey

2 tablespoons olive oil
1 pound green beans, trimmed and blanched
1 red pepper, julienned
4 slices bacon, fried crisp and crumbled
1/4 cup chopped pecans, toasted
Salt and pepper

Heat olive oil in saucepan. Add beans, pepper, bacon and pecans. Sauté over medium-high heat until peppers are tender. Season with salt and pepper.

Serve with Pork Chops with Apple Glaze (page 71), Apple Raisin Chutney (page 35) and Buttermilk Mashers (page 39).

Makes 4 to 6 servings.

Polaris Grill
TUNA SALAD
Recipe of Chef Tom A. Callaghan

1	6-ounce can tuna, drained
1 1/2	tablespoons diced white onion
1/4	cup peeled, seeded and diced cucumber
1/2	teaspoon minced fresh chives
1/3	cup mayonnaise
	Salt and pepper

Mix together all ingredients. Chill until ready to serve.

Makes 2 servings.

Entrees

The Leatherlips Statue at Scioto Park

Trattoria Roma
BUCATINI AMATRICIANA
Recipe of Chef Jamie George

2	tablespoons olive oil
1	tablespoon chopped fresh sage
1	tablespoon chopped fresh rosemary
1/4	teaspoon red pepper flakes
1/2	cup chopped pancetta (Italian bacon)*
1	yellow onion, minced
4	garlic cloves, chopped
1	tablespoon chopped fresh basil
1	cup white wine
4	cups crushed tomatoes
	Coarse salt
	Cracked black pepper
1	pound bucatini pasta*

In large pan sauté in olive oil, the sage, rosemary, red pepper flakes and pancetta for 2 to 3 minutes. Add onion and garlic ; cook until translucent. Stir in basil. Deglaze with wine. Add tomatoes and simmer for 10 to 15 minutes or until sauce is desired consistency. Season with salt and pepper. Cook pasta al dente. Top with sauce.

Makes 4 servings.

* This product is available at Carfagna's.

Firdous

CHICKEN KABOB
Recipe of Chef Nasir Latif

6 boneless, skinless chicken breasts
Salt
1 lemon

1	tablespoon paprika	4-5	garlic cloves, minced
1/4	teaspoon pepper	2	tablespoons vinegar
1/4	teaspoon allspice		Pinch oregano
	Pinch cumin	1	cup vegetable oil
	Pinch nutmeg		Salt

Vegetables for grilling (green peppers, onions, red peppers, cherry tomatoes, mushrooms, etc.)

On day before serving, rinse chicken with cold water. Lightly salt chicken and squeeze fresh lemon juice over it. Let sit for 10 minutes. Rinse again.

To prepare marinade, in large bowl combine remaining ingredients except vegetables for grilling. Whisk together thoroughly. Set aside.

Cut chicken into cubes. Place cubes in marinade and refrigerate overnight for best flavor.

The following day, prepare skewers, alternating chicken cubes with vegetables. Grill until chicken is fully cooked.

Makes 4 to 6 servings.

Polaris Grill
CRAB CAKES WITH CREOLE MUSTARD SAUCE
Recipe of Chef Tom A. Callaghan

1	egg
2	tablespoons mayonnaise
1 1/2	teaspoons minced parsley
1/2	teaspoon yellow mustard
	Pinch cayenne pepper
	Pinch white pepper
1/4	teaspoon salt
	Pinch Old Bay Seasoning
	Pinch black pepper
12	ounces lump crabmeat, drained
1 1/2	tablespoons finely ground saltines
1/2	cup white wine
3	whole black peppercorns
3/4	teaspoon minced shallots
1	bay leaf
3/4	teaspoon horseradish
6	tablespoons heavy cream
1/4	cup unsalted butter, room temperature
3/4	teaspoon stone ground mustard
3/4	teaspoon Dijon mustard
	Pinch Old Bay Seasoning
	Salt and pepper
	Pinch ground cayenne pepper

In medium bowl, combine thoroughly first 9 ingredients. Gently fold in crabmeat. Gently fold in saltines. Cover and refrigerate for one hour.

While crab mixture chills, prepare Creole mustard sauce. Place wine, peppercorns, shallots, bay leaf and horseradish in medium saucepan and simmer to reduce by half. Add cream and simmer until it starts to thicken. Whisk in butter a tablespoon at a time until desired consistency. Remove bay leaf and peppercorns. Add remaining ingredients. Set aside.

Heat griddle with small amount of butter on it. Form crab mixture into 4 patties and pan-fry until golden brown on both sides. Serve with Creole mustard sauce.

Makes 2 servings.

Trattoria Roma

Fettuccine ai Funghi
Porcini Gorgonzola
Recipe of Chef Jamie George

1	yellow onion, finely chopped
1 1/2	tablespoons finely chopped fresh sage
1 1/2	tablespoons finely chopped fresh rosemary
4	garlic cloves, finely chopped
1	ounce dried porcini mushrooms*, soaked in water for 15 minutes, drained and sliced
2	cups sliced mushrooms
2	tablespoons olive oil
1	tablespoon butter
2	cups sherry wine
3	tablespoons finely chopped fresh parsley
3	tablespoons finely chopped fresh basil
3	tablespoons balsamic vinegar
3	cups prepared vegetable broth or chicken broth
1	quart heavy whipping cream
	Salt and pepper
1	pound spinach-flavored fettuccine, cooked
1	cup crumbled Gorgonzola cheese

In large pan, sauté onion, sage, rosemary, garlic, and both kinds of mushrooms in olive oil and butter until mushrooms are soft. Deglaze with sherry. Add parsley, basil, vinegar, broth and cream. Simmer for approximately 25 minutes or until desired consistency, stirring occasionally. Season with salt

61

and pepper. Toss with pasta and Gorgonzola cheese.

Makes 4 servings.
* This product is available at Carfagna's.

Scioto River

Martini Italian Bistro

LASAGNA

Recipe of Chef Rick Lindeboom

1 1/4	pounds ground Italian hot sausage
2	tablespoons olive oil
1	small carrot, chopped
1	stalk celery, chopped
1	medium onion, chopped
8	ounces tomato paste
2	cups water
1 1/2	teaspoons minced garlic
3/4	teaspoon chopped fresh rosemary
3/4	teaspoon chopped fresh basil
3/4	teaspoon chopped fresh parsley
1	pound Ricotta cheese
3/4	cup grated Asiago cheese
1/3	cup grated Parmesan cheese
1/3	cup heavy cream
1 1/2	teaspoons chopped fresh basil
1 1/2	teaspoons chopped fresh rosemary
1 1/2	teaspoons chopped fresh oregano
1 1/2	teaspoons chopped fresh parsley
1	onion, diced
1/4	cup olive oil
1/4	cup minced garlic
1 1/2	teaspoons chopped fresh oregano
1 1/2	teaspoons chopped fresh thyme
2	tablespoons chopped fresh basil

2	tablespoons chopped fresh parsley
1	tablespoon sugar
1	tablespoon salt
1½	teaspoons pepper
1	teaspoon ground fennel
1	28-ounce can stewed tomatoes
1	6-ounce can tomato paste
1	cup water
1	16-ounce box lasagna noodles
1	pound Provolone cheese, shredded

Brown sausage; drain fat. Set aside.

In large pan, in 2 tablespoons olive oil, sauté carrots, celery and onion for 8 to 10 minutes or until carrots begin to soften. Add sausage to pan. Add 8 ounces tomato paste and water. Add 1½ teaspoons garlic, ¾ teaspoon rosemary, ¾ teaspoon basil and ¾ teaspoon parsley. Simmer until reduced and thick, about 10 minutes.

In bowl, combine cheeses, cream, 1½ teaspoons basil, 1½ teaspoons rosemary, 1½ teaspoons oregano and 1½ teaspoons parsley. Set aside.

To make marinara sauce, sauté onion in olive oil until translucent. Add garlic and sauté an additional 2 minutes. Add remaining ingredients (except noodles and Provolone) and simmer for 25 to 30 minutes, adding water as needed. Continue stirring to break up tomatoes until sauce is thick.

Cook lasagna noodles according to package directions.

Preheat oven to 400°. This recipe makes enough lasagna for one 9 x 13-inch pan and one 9 x 9-inch pan. (You can freeze one for later.) Layer in both pans, lasagna noodles, cheese filling, sausage filling, another layer of lasagna noodles, marinara sauce and Provolone cheese. Repeat. Cover pans with foil. Bake for 30 minutes. Bake uncovered for 5 to 10 minutes.

Makes one 9 x 13-inch pan and one 9 x 9-inch pan.

The Ocean Exhibit at C.O.S.I.

Cap City Diner
MEATLOAF
Recipe of Chef Jimmy Mohammed

1 1/2	cups ketchup
1	tablespoon Worcestershire sauce
1/4	teaspoon garlic powder
2 1/4	teaspoons molasses
6	tablespoons brown sugar
3/4	teaspoon salt
	Pinch cayenne pepper
1	teaspoon cider vinegar
6	tablespoons water
2	tablespoons honey
1	tablespoon fresh orange juice
1/4	teaspoon black pepper
2	cups sliced shiitake mushrooms
2	tablespoons diced white onion
1	tablespoon olive oil
1	pound ground beef
4	ounces ground veal (optional)
10	ounces ground pork
1	egg
3/4	cup bread crumbs
1 1/2	teaspoons chopped fresh parsley
1/2	teaspoon chopped fresh thyme
1/2	teaspoon chopped fresh sage
2 1/4	teaspoons minced garlic

2 1/4   teaspoons heavy cream
 3/4   teaspoon Worcestershire sauce
  1   teaspoon salt
  1   teaspoon pepper

To make barbecue sauce, in medium saucepan combine first 12 ingredients. Stir well. Simmer for 20 minutes. Allow to cool.

Preheat oven to 325°.

In skillet, sauté mushrooms and onion in olive oil until tender. Set aside.

In large bowl, combine meats, egg, bread crumbs, herbs, garlic and cream. Mix well. Add mushrooms and onions. Add 2 tablespoons of previously prepared barbecue sauce. Add remaining ingredients and mix thoroughly.

Place mixture in loaf pan, pushing down firmly to pack meat into place. Cover with foil. Bake for 50 to 60 minutes. Remove foil and cover meatloaf with desired amount of barbecue sauce. Cook uncovered for an additional 10 to 15 minutes.

Serve with barbecue sauce.

Makes 8 servings.

Red Door Tavern
OGLIO OLEO
Recipe of Chef Sean Lorigan

1	teaspoon minced garlic
1/4	cup olive oil
2	ounces prosciutto (Italian ham), finely chopped
4	ounces chicken breast, cubed
1/2	cup sliced mushrooms
8	ounces angel hair pasta, cooked
	Salt and pepper

In heavy pan, sauté garlic in oil until light brown. Add ham, chicken and mushrooms and cook thoroughly. Remove from heat. Toss with pasta. Season with salt and pepper.

Makes 1 to 2 servings.

Red Door Tavern
O'LONERGAN'S ALFREDO
Recipe of Chef Sean Lorigan

1 tablespoon butter
1 quart heavy cream
1 pound finely grated Parmesan cheese
1 teaspoon nutmeg
  Fettuccine noodles, cooked

Heat butter in large heavy pot. Add cream and bring to low boil. Slowly add cheese, mixing constantly until creamy, semi-thick consistency. Blend in nutmeg. Serve immediately on fettuccine noodles.

Makes 8 to 12 servings.

Shaw's Inn
Pan-Fried Rib Eye Steak with Balsamic Glaze
Recipe of Chef Denise Denman

2	tablespoons unsalted butter
4	rib eye steaks, about ½-inch thick
1	large shallot, minced
½	cup balsamic vinegar
3	tablespoons unsalted butter
	Salt
	Freshly ground black pepper

In large heavy skillet over medium-high heat, melt 2 tablespoons of butter and sauté steaks 2 to 3 minutes per side for rare, or to desired doneness. Remove steaks to serving platter.

Add shallot to skillet and cook for 30 seconds. Pour in vinegar and boil until reduced to 2 tablespoons. Remove pan from heat; whisk in remaining butter and season with salt and pepper.

Pour sauce over steaks and serve immediately.

Makes 4 servings.

Cap City Diner
PORK CHOPS WITH APPLE GLAZE
Recipe of Chef Brian Hershey

1	orange
2	cups apple cider
1/2	cup honey
1	teaspoon cracked black pepper
4	rib pork chops*
3	tablespoons oil

Grate peel from orange and mince peel finely. Squeeze juice from orange into saucepan. Add minced orange peel, cider, honey and pepper. Stir and simmer until liquid is reduced by half. Set aside.

Preheat oven to 350°.

In large frying pan, sear pork chops over medium heat in oil until golden brown on both sides. Place chops in oven-safe pan. Pour small amount of apple glaze over pork chops. Bake in oven for 4 to 5 minutes per side or until done. Top with more apple glaze.

Serve with Apple Raisin Chutney (page 35), Buttermilk Mashers (page 39) and Skillet Beans (page 53).

Makes 4 servings.

* Cap City uses 3-inch double-rib chops.

Engine House No. 5
POTATO ENCRUSTED WHITEFISH
Recipe of Chef Rocky

4   Idaho potatoes, peeled and coarsely grated
      Juice of one lemon

4   8-ounce boneless whitefish fillets
      Salt and pepper
1/2   cup olive oil

Place potatoes in small bowl and toss with lemon juice to keep potatoes from turning brown. Set aside.

Season fish lightly with salt and pepper.

Spread potatoes evenly, about 1/4-inch thick, over the flesh side of the fillets.

Add olive oil to large frying pan and place on high. When pan is hot, place fish in pan potato side down, and cook for 5 to 6 minutes or until potatoes are well browned and crispy.

Turn fillets over and continue cooking for 2 more minutes or until desired doneness.

Remove fish from pan and place on platter. Season to taste.

Makes 4 servings.

ROAST LEG OF LAMB*
Recipe of Chef Nasir Latif

Small boneless leg of spring lamb
Olive oil

2	tablespoons olive oil
1/2	teaspoon pepper
	Pinch nutmeg
	Pinch onion powder
10	bay leaves
	Pinch oregano
1	box wild rice
1/2	cup pine nuts
1 1/2	teaspoons olive oil
2	cups water

The day before serving, cut lamb open down center of leg. Using sharp knife, cut each side of leg away from center to create pocket for rice stuffing. Rinse leg with cold water. Place in baking dish. Cover inside and outside with olive oil. Set aside.

In separate bowl, combine 2 tablespoons olive oil and remaining spices. Mix well. Rub inside and outside of lamb with seasonings. Cover dish and refrigerate overnight.

The next day, prepare wild rice according to directions on package. Set aside.

Sauté pine nuts in 1 1/2 teaspoons olive oil until golden

brown. Add to rice. Mix well.

Remove lamb from baking dish and place on sheet of aluminum foil. Stuff leg of lamb with rice. Close pocket. Wrap entire leg of lamb with foil. Place in clean baking dish. Pour water into dish. If desired, vegetables (carrots, potatoes, onions, etc.) can be added to pan and roasted with meat.

Bake at 375° for at least 2 ¹/₂ hours or until tender. Remove bay leaves before serving.

Makes 4 servings.
*This is a favorite of the Grumpy Gourmet (February 2000).

Columbus Zoo

Michael Dominic's Steak and Seafood

Scallops Dominic with Dominic Sauce

Recipe of Chef Nick Hutras

1 1/2	teaspoons olive oil
1	tablespoon chopped red onion
1	tablespoon chopped green pepper
1/3	cup sliced fresh mushrooms
3/4	teaspoon minced garlic
1 1/2	tablespoons Chablis
3/4	teaspoon lemon juice
1	cup milk
1	cup heavy cream
1/3	cup clam juice
1/4	cup chicken broth
	Dash Tabasco sauce
1/4	teaspoon dry mustard
	Dash cayenne pepper
1/4	teaspoon thyme
1	tablespoon grated Parmesan cheese
1/4	cup butter
1/4	cup flour
1/4	cup water
2	pounds scallops
	Salt and pepper
2	tablespoons butter

Seasoned bread crumbs
Chopped fresh parsley

In olive oil, sauté onion, green pepper, mushrooms and garlic for 5 minutes. Add Chablis and lemon juice. Cook until reduced by half. Stir in milk and cream. Add clam juice, chicken broth, Tabasco, dry mustard, cayenne pepper, thyme and cheese. Cook until sauce begins to boil. Reduce heat and simmer 2 to 3 minutes.

Prepare roux by melting butter in small saucepan. Stir in flour. Add water until it becomes a paste.

Add roux to sauce and whisk until smooth. When sauce thickens, remove from heat. Set aside.

To prepare scallops, place in casserole dish. Season with salt and pepper. Sprinkle with a few drops of water and melted butter. Broil for 6 to 8 minutes. Remove from oven. Cover scallops with desired amount of sauce. Sprinkle with seasoned bread crumbs. Broil until golden.

Garnish with parsley.

Makes 4 servings.

Alana's
SHANGHAI RIBS
Recipe of Chef Alana Shock

2	pounds spare ribs
1/4	cup soy sauce
2	tablespoons sugar
2	tablespoons hoisin sauce
2	tablespoons pale dry sherry
1	teaspoon minced garlic
1	teaspoon ground ginger
2	tablespoons chicken stock or water

Place ribs in shallow oven-safe pan.

In bowl, mix remaining ingredients. Pour over ribs and marinate 3 to 4 hours, turning once every hour.

Cover pan tightly and cook for 45 minutes at 375°. Uncover and baste. Bake at 425° for 40 minutes or until tender.

Makes 4 servings.

Engine House No. 5
SHRIMP DANIELLE
Recipe of Chef Larry

40	jumbo shrimp, uncooked
	Salt
1	cup flour
	Olive oil
1/2	cup butter or margarine, softened
1	tablespoon plus 1 teaspoon dry white wine, room temperature
	Pinch salt
	Pinch pepper
1/4	teaspoon minced garlic
1/2	teaspoon minced anchovies
1 1/2	teaspoons finely chopped parsley
1 1/2	teaspoons finely chopped green pepper
1 1/2	teaspoons finely chopped pimientos
1/4	cup sliced almonds, toasted

Peel and devein shrimp, leaving tail. Season shrimp with salt. Dust shrimp lightly with flour and arrange tightly in rows on baking sheet with sides touching. Brush with oil. Set aside.

In mixer, blend together butter, wine, salt, pepper, garlic and anchovies. Add parsley, green pepper and pimientos; combine thoroughly. Evenly distribute butter mixture over shrimp.

Broil shrimp on lower rack in oven for approximately 4 minutes on each side until butter melts and shrimp are lightly browned.

Portion shrimp onto 4 plates and garnish with toasted almonds.

Makes 4 servings.

Ohio State Football

Red Door Tavern
SIRLOIN TIPS
Recipe of Chef Sean Lorigan

6	ounces sirloin steak, cubed
1	small onion, diced
1/4	green pepper, diced
1/4	red pepper, diced
1	redskin potato, thinly sliced
2	tablespoons oil
2	slices garlic bread, toasted
1	cup beef gravy with mushrooms, heated through
	Salt and pepper

In heavy skillet, sauté steak and vegetables in oil to desired doneness. Place on top of garlic bread and smother with gravy. Season wth salt and pepper.

Makes 1 to 2 servings.

Siam Restaurant
THAI PASTA
Recipe of Chef John Tai

5 1/2	ounces rice noodles*
1	tablespoon olive oil
6	shrimp
1	egg
1/2	teaspoon curry powder
1	tablespoon fish sauce
1	teaspoon sugar
1	pinch white pepper
1 1/2	tablespoons minced green onion
1 1/2	tablespoons minced red pepper
1 1/2	tablespoons minced green pepper
2	tablespoons minced white onion
2	cups bean sprouts

In medium bowl, cover rice noodles with cold water and soak for at least 30 minutes.

Place olive oil in wok and heat to medium high. Stir-fry shrimp until done. Break egg over shrimp and stir-fry. Drain water from noodles and add noodles to wok. Stir curry powder into mixture and continue cooking for 1 minute. Stir in fish sauce, sugar and white pepper. Add remaining ingredients and stir-fry briefly until heated through.

Makes 1 serving.

* This product is available at Chinese markets.

Martini Italian Bistro
TUNA WITH CHOPPED HERBS
Recipe of Chef Rick Lindeboom

1 teaspoon chopped fresh rosemary
1 teaspoon chopped fresh sage
1 teaspoon chopped fresh thyme
1 teaspoon chopped fresh oregano
4 6-ounce tuna steaks
   Olive oil

Combine spices. Coat tuna with spice mixture. In heavy pan, sear tuna in small amount of oil for 2 minutes on each side or to desired doneness.

Serve with Ratatouille (page 48).

Makes 4 servings.

Cameron's
WALNUT ENCRUSTED SALMON
Recipe of Chef Fred Braun

1 orange
1 lemon
1 lime

1 cup olive oil

6 6-ounce fresh, skinless salmon fillets

2 oranges
1 shallot, minced
1¼ cups olive oil
1 tablespoon cracked black peppercorns
   Salt

1 cup finely chopped walnuts
½ cup bread crumbs
2 tablespoons olive oil

To make marinade, grate peel from orange, lemon and lime. Mince peel finely. Squeeze juice from all three fruits into small bowl. Stir in minced peel and 1 cup olive oil. Place salmon in baking dish. Pour fruit marinade over salmon and refrigerate for 4 hours.

To prepare sauce for salmon (orange mignonette), grate peel from 2 oranges. Mince peel finely. Squeeze juice from oranges into bowl. Blend in minced orange peel and shallot. Whisk in olive oil. Add peppercorns and salt. Set aside.

Preheat oven to 400°.

Mix together walnuts and bread crumbs. Slowly add olive oil to form moist, crumbly crust for salmon. Set aside.

Heat small amount of olive oil in frying pan. Sear salmon top side down until browned. Discard marinade. Turn salmon over and place in baking dish. Top with walnut mixture. Place in oven and bake for 5 to 6 minutes until topping is browned or to desired doneness.

When done, place salmon on Celeriac Mashed Potatoes (page 40). Surround salmon/potatoes with Red Onion, Celery and Apple Compote (page 49). Drizzle with orange mignonette.

Makes 6 servings.

DESSERTS

Worthington Arts Festival

Barcelona

APPLE PEAR PIE
Recipe of Chef Paul Yow

3   Granny Smith apples
2   pears

1/4   cup flour
3/4   cup granulated sugar
1   tablespoon lemon juice
1/4   teaspoon cinnamon
1   egg, slightly beaten

1   prepared 9-inch pie shell

1/2   cup butter
1   cup flour
3/4   cup brown sugar
1/2   cup granulated sugar

Preheat oven to 350°.

Peel, core and slice apples and pears. Set aside.

Combine next 5 ingredients. Add apples and pears; blend until coated. Place filling into pie shell.

To make streusel topping, combine remaining ingredients in bowl and blend with pastry cutter until pieces are the size of peas. Sprinkle over top of pie, making sure all apples and pears are completely covered.

Bake at 350° for 50 to 60 minutes.

Makes 8 to 10 servings.

Taj Palace

BADAMEE KHEER
(INDIAN RICE PUDDING)
Recipe of Chef Jinder Singh

1   cup basmati rice
2   quarts milk
1 1/2   cups sugar
      Almonds

Place rice in bowl and cover with water. Soak 15 minutes. In saucepan bring milk and sugar to boil. Immediately reduce heat and simmer 2 to 3 minutes. Drain rice. Add rice to milk mixture and continue to simmer 35 to 40 minutes or until liquid has been reduced and mixture is the consistency of pudding. Stir often to prevent sticking. Allow pudding to cool. Top with almonds.

Makes 6 to 8 servings.

*F*irdous

BAKLAVA
Recipe of Chef Nasir Latif

1   16-ounce package phyllo dough

1   tablespoon butter, softened

4   cups finely chopped walnuts*

1 1/2   cups honey

1/2   cup butter, melted

2   cups sugar

1   cup water

1 1/2   teaspoons lemon juice

Remove phyllo dough from freezer and thaw according to directions on package. Do not unwrap phyllo.

For filling, combine 1 tablespoon butter, walnuts and honey. Mix well and set aside.

Grease 8 x 8-inch baking dish. Set aside.

Once dough is thawed, remove from plastic. Carefully unroll phyllo sheets onto smooth, dry surface. Cut an 8 x 8-inch section from phyllo sheets. Remove excess dough. Reroll; wrap securely in plastic wrap and refrigerate or refreeze.

Take 1 sheet of phyllo dough and place it on bottom of prepared pan. Brush entire surface with melted butter. Repeat this process 9 times. Next, place walnut and honey mixture over the 10 layers of dough, spreading mixture evenly to all sides of pan. Continue to layer pan with remaining sheets of phyllo dough, brushing melted butter between each layer, ending with butter on top.

Preheat oven to 350°.

Cut baklava before baking. Using sharp knife, cut diagonal line connecting opposite corners. Reverse the diagonal and connect the second set of corners. Move knife out from diagonal guidelines in 1-inch increments, using a ruler if desired to obtain diamond-shaped pieces.

Bake for 30 to 45 minutes, watching closely until it turns golden brown in color. Remove from oven and cool to room temperature.

In medium saucepan over medium heat, combine sugar and water. Stir until sugar is dissolved. Bring just to boil and reduce to low heat. Continue to cook until syrup begins to thicken, about 30 to 45 minutes, stirring frequently. Blend in lemon. Watch very carefully for syrup to change to a light yellow color. Once it begins to change, immediately remove from heat. Do not overcook.

Pour hot syrup over cooled baklava. Cool completely before serving.

Makes 10 to 15 servings.

*Pistachios, cashews or pecans may be substituted for walnuts.

Mitchell's Steak House
BANANA BREAD PUDDING CUSTARD
Recipe of Chef David Dovell

1/4	cup egg yolks (about 4)
3	tablespoons granulated sugar
1 1/2	cups heavy cream
1/8	teaspoon vanilla
1	cup half-and-half
1/8	teaspoon vanilla
3	egg yolks
1/4	cup granulated sugar
2	ounces white chocolate, finely chopped
1	tablespoon dark rum
1	tablespoon banana liqueur (or extract)
1	tablespoon chopped hazelnuts
4	slices day-old white bread, cut into 1/2-inch pieces

Vanilla ice cream
Caramel sauce
Hazelnuts
Mint sprigs
Powdered sugar

To make custard, whisk together 1/4 cup egg yolks and 3 tablespoons sugar in bowl. Set aside.

In saucepan, bring heavy cream and 1/8 teaspoon vanilla to simmer. Remove from heat. Blend small amount of cream into egg yolk mixture. Continue to add cream until half has been added. Add egg mixture back into saucepan. Return pan to heat and cook over low heat for 1 minute, stirring constantly. Strain mixture through fine strainer. Refrigerate.

To make vanilla sauce, heat half-and-half and $1/8$ teaspoon vanilla in saucepan until it simmers. Remove from heat. In bowl, whisk together 3 egg yolks and sugar. Using same process as above, gradually pour half of warm cream into yolks and then return mixture to saucepan, stirring constantly. Cook until thick. Chill.

In large bowl, mix together white chocolate, previously made custard, rum, banana flavoring and 1 tablespoon hazelnuts. Add bread and mix together. Most of the liquid should be absorbed but mixture should still be somewhat soupy.

Butter 4 individual oven-safe dishes and coat lightly with sugar. Divide bread mixture into cups. Bake in water bath covered with foil at 350° for 30 minutes. Uncover and continue to bake until custard is set and tops are golden brown.

Top each pudding with vanilla ice cream, caramel sauce and previously made vanilla sauce. Garnish with hazelnuts, mint sprigs and powdered sugar. Serve immediately.

Makes 4 servings.

The River Club
BANANAS FOSTER
Chef Michael Wolf

1/4 cup butter

4 bananas, firm (not overly ripe)

1/3 cup brown sugar

2 tablespoons sliced almonds

2 tablespoons dark rum, warm

4 scoops vanilla ice cream

In non-stick pan, melt butter over medium heat. While butter is melting, slice bananas 1/4- to 1/2-inch thick. Add bananas, sugar and almonds to pan. Sauté 3 minutes without turning. Turn bananas once and sauté briefly until golden brown. Pour warm rum over bananas and flame off carefully. Evenly distribute bananas over 4 servings of ice cream and serve immediately.

Makes 4 servings.

Spagio

BERRY BREAD PUDDING
Recipe of Chef Hubert Seifert

4	cups cubed bread (challah, brioche or raisin)	3/4	cup granulated sugar
1	cup blueberries	1 1/2	cups milk
3/4	cup raspberries	1 1/2	teaspoons vanilla
3	large eggs	1/2	teaspoon nutmeg
1	large egg yolk		Confectioners sugar
			Whipped cream

Place bread cubes and both berries in greased 8 x 8-inch baking dish. Set aside.

In medium bowl, beat whole eggs and egg yolk with mixer until frothy. Add sugar and beat until thick, 3 to 4 minutes. Reduce speed of mixer and blend in milk, vanilla and nutmeg.

Ladle mixture over bread and berries. Let sit for 45 minutes to an hour so bread can absorb custard.

Preheat oven to 375°.

Place baking dish in water bath. Bake for 30 minutes. Using wooden spoon, push bread down so that custard rises to top. Spoon custard over top of bread pudding. Bake an additional 5 minutes.

Remove from oven and let cool for 10 to 15 minutes.

Dust with confectioners sugar and serve with whipped cream.

Makes 6 to 8 servings.

Brookside Golf and Country Club
CHOCOLATE LAVA CAKE
Recipe of Chef Jay Yardley

1/2   cup butter
6   ounces bittersweet or semi-sweet chocolate
     Pinch salt

2   eggs
2   egg yolks
1/2   cup sugar
2   tablespoons flour

     Graeter's black raspberry chocolate chip ice cream

In double boiler, melt butter and chocolate. Add salt. Remove from heat.

In separate bowl, combine eggs, yolks and sugar. Fold in chocolate mixture. Fold in flour.

Pour into 4 greased and floured 8-ounce oven-safe dishes. Bake at 450° for 13 to 15 minutes. Outer edges should be firm. Centers should be wet. Let stand for 2 minutes prior to serving. Serve with Graeter's black raspberry chocolate chip ice cream.

Makes 4 servings.

Seven Stars at The Worthington Inn
CRÈME BRULÉE
Recipe of Chef Joseph M. Harris

4	egg yolks	Granulated sugar
1/3	cup brown sugar	Fresh berries
1 1/4	teaspoons vanilla	Powdered sugar
3 1/2	cups heavy cream	

Preheat oven to 350°.

In medium bowl, using mixer thoroughly combine yolks and brown sugar. Set aside.

In saucepan, heat vanilla and cream just to scalding point. Remove from heat. Gradually pour vanilla/cream into egg mixture, stirring constantly.

Pour into individual oven-safe dishes, making sure liquid is less than one inch deep.

Place dishes in large baking pan and add hot water around dishes to reach halfway up the sides, being careful not to get any water into crème brulée.

Bake for about 30 to 45 minutes, occasionally checking for doneness. Brulées are done when they have a light firmness and resemble jello when shaken. Do not brown tops.

Once done, remove from water bath and chill.

To serve, sprinkle each dish with heavy coating of sugar. Brown under broiler. Garnish with berries and sprinkle with powdered sugar.

Makes 8 to 10 servings, depending on size of dish.

Cap City Diner
DEEP DISH GRANNY APPLE PIE
Recipe of Chef Jimmy Mohammed

1/4	cup slivered almonds
2 1/4	cups flour
1 1/2	tablespoons sugar
3/4	teaspoon salt
6	ounces butter, cubed
1/4	cup ice water
10	Granny Smith apples, peeled and sliced
1	cup sugar
6	tablespoons flour
1 1/4	teaspoons cinnamon
1/2	teaspoon nutmeg
2	tablespoons lemon juice
1	cup flour
1/2	cup sugar
1/2	cup cold butter, cubed
	Vanilla ice cream
	Caramel sauce

Using food processor, grind almonds to fine grain. Transfer to mixing bowl and blend in flour, 1 1/2 tablespoons sugar and salt. Using pastry cutter, blend in butter until pea-sized. Add water and blend by hand until incorporated, handling as little as possible.

To make apple filling, in large bowl combine thoroughly

next 6 ingredients.

To make streusel topping, in medium bowl combine flour and sugar. Add cubed butter and work with hands until crumbly. Set aside.

Preheat oven to 350°.

Press almond dough onto bottom and sides of 10-inch spring-form pan. The crust should be $1/4$- to $1/2$-inch thick.

Spoon apple filling into crust.

Top with streusel, being sure to completely cover all apples.

Place on parchment-lined tray and bake for $1 1/2$ to 2 hours, or until apples are tender.

Serve with vanilla ice cream and caramel sauce.

Makes 8 servings.

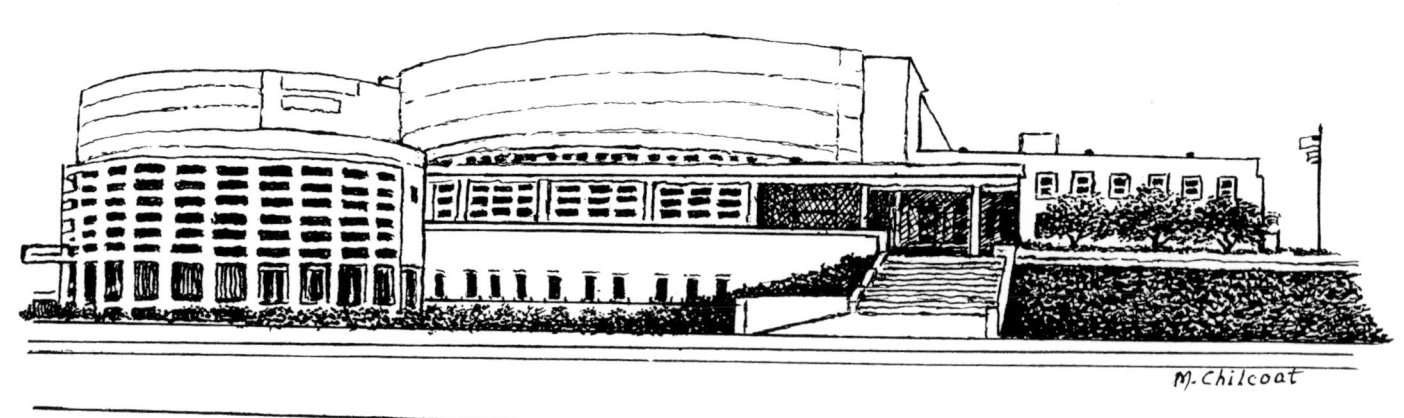

Veteran's Memorial

La Chatelaine
FRUIT TART WITH SUGAR DOUGH
Recipe of Chef Tad Wielezynski

1 1/4	cups flour
1 1/2	tablespoons sugar
1/4	teaspoon salt
1/2	cup cold unsalted butter cut into small pieces
1	egg yolk, slightly beaten
2-3	tablespoons ice water
1	cup milk
1/2	teaspoon vanilla
1/4	cup sugar
1	tablespoon sugar
3	egg yolks
1	tablespoon cornstarch
1	tablespoon flour
1	cup heavy cream

Fruit (Strawberries, raspberries, mandarin oranges, etc.)

Place flour, 1 1/2 tablespoons sugar and salt in food processor. Add butter pieces and process 10 seconds. Add yolk and water a little at a time until dough can be formed into ball but is not wet or sticky.* Form ball and cover with plastic wrap. Refrigerate for one hour.

Lightly butter or spray with cooking spray one 9-inch pie pan. Remove dough from plastic wrap and roll out to 1/8-inch thick on lightly floured board. Place dough in pan. Trim excess dough from edges. Flute edges if desired.

Cover dough with foil, pressing onto bottom and edges. Bake for 18 minutes at 375°. Remove foil and bake another 5 to 7 minutes or until crust is lightly browned. Remove from oven. Allow to cool completely.

In saucepan, scald milk, vanilla and $1/4$ cup sugar. Immediately remove from heat.

In separate bowl, beat 1 tablespoon sugar with egg yolks, cornstarch and flour. Add half of milk mixture to eggs, stirring constantly. Return milk/eggs to saucepan. Over medium heat, bring mixture to boil, stirring constantly. Reduce heat and cook 1 minute. Remove from heat. Allow to cool slightly. Stir. Cover with plastic wrap and let cool completely.

Whip cream. Fold into pudding mixture. Pour into cooled pie crust. Arrange fruit on top. Chill until ready to serve.

Makes one 9-inch tart.

* This process can also be done the traditional way with pastry cutter.

Biddie's Coach House
"Hard to Believe"
Low-Fat Fruit Cobbler
Recipe of Proprietor Mary Marsalka

16	ounces frozen fruit
2	cups flour
2	cups sugar
2	teaspoons baking powder
1	12-ounce can evaporated milk

Whipped topping

Coat 9 x 13-inch pan with cooking spray. Spread frozen fruit in bottom of pan.

Combine remaining ingredients except whipped topping and pour over fruit. Bake at 350° for 45 minutes to 1 hour or until toothpick inserted in middle comes out clean. Serve warm and top with whipped topping.

Makes 10 to 12 servings.

Spagio

INDIVIDUAL CHOCOLATE SOUFFLÉ CAKES

Recipe of Chef Hubert Seifert

5 1/2   ounces bittersweet chocolate, cut into small pieces
1/2   cup plus 1 tablespoon unsalted butter

3   large eggs
3   large egg yolks
1/3   cup granulated sugar
5   tablespoons flour

Confectioners sugar

Preheat oven to 375°. Grease six 8-ounce oven-safe dishes.

Over low heat in top of double boiler, combine chocolate and butter. Stir until melted. Remove from heat.

In bowl, beat next 3 ingredients with mixer for about 5 minutes. Add flour and blend well.

Add chocolate and mix briefly.

Divide mixture between dishes.

Bake for 10 to 12 minutes. The outside edges should be set, but the center soft. Do not over-bake.

Remove from oven and dust with confectioners sugar.

Makes 6 servings.

Katzinger's
JUST PLAIN OLD-FASHIONED
CHOCOLATE CAKE
Recipe of Owner Diane Warren

1/2	cup butter, softened
1	cup granulated sugar
1	cup brown sugar
2	eggs
1	cup brewed coffee
1/2	cup hot tap water
1/2	cup unsweetened cocoa powder
1 3/4	cups flour
1	teaspoon baking soda
1 1/2	teaspoons vanilla
3	egg yolks
1 1/4	cups semi-sweet chocolate chips
3	tablespoons water
3/4	cup granulated sugar
1	cup butter

In large bowl, using mixer blend together 1/2 cup butter and first 2 sugars. With mixer on low setting, add next 7 ingredients, one at a time, waiting until each is fully incorporated before adding the next. (The batter will be somewhat thin.)

Pour batter evenly into 3 well-greased 8- or 9-inch round cake pans.

Bake at 350° for approximately 18 to 20 minutes or until toothpick inserted in center comes out clean.

Allow to cool.

To prepare frosting, place egg yolks and chocolate chips in mixing bowl. Set aside.

In saucepan over high heat, combine water and sugar. Cook briefly until sugar is completely dissolved and mixture forms simple syrup.

Pour warm sugar mixture over eggs and chocolate. With mixer, blend until smooth.

Add butter a little at a time until all butter has been added. Mix until smooth and creamy.

Chill frosting about 30 minutes before icing cake.

Makes 12 to 16 servings.

North Market

Barcelona
MACAROONS
Recipe of Chef Paul Yow

1	cup egg whites
2 1/2	cups sugar
2	tablespoons honey
2	teaspoons vanilla
15	ounces shredded coconut
1 1/4	cups flour

In double boiler over medium heat, whisk together first 4 ingredients until sugar dissolves and mixture thins. Remove from heat and add last 2 ingredients. Mix well. Refrigerate until mixture firms, about one hour.

Preheat oven to 300°. Drop by tablespoons on parchment-lined cookie sheet.

Bake for 20 to 25 minutes, or until golden brown.

Makes approximately 3 dozen cookies.

Cameron's
MEYER LEMON GRATIN
Recipe of Chef Fred Braun

2	lemons
1/2	orange
2	pounds cream cheese
1 3/4	cups sugar
3	egg yolks
1 1/2	teaspoons vanilla
3/4	cup heavy cream, whipped
2	teaspoons sour cream
3	egg whites, whipped to form stiff peaks
1	lemon
1	cup half-and-half
6	tablespoons sugar
3	egg yolks

Preheat oven to 300°. Spray six 10-ounce oven-safe dishes with vegetable spray. Coat completely with sugar.

Grate peel from lemons and 1/2 orange. Mince peel finely and set aside. Squeeze juice from lemons and orange and set aside.

Using mixer, in large bowl combine cream cheese, 1 3/4 cups sugar, minced lemon peel and minced orange peel.

In separate bowl, combine lemon and orange juices, 3 egg yolks and vanilla. Add to cream cheese mixture and blend thoroughly.

Fold in whipped cream and sour cream.

Fold in whipped egg whites until blended.

Evenly divide mixture into prepared dishes.

Place filled dishes into baking pan. Fill pan with $^1/_2$ inch hot water, being careful not to spill water into filled cups.

Bake at 300° for 30 minutes. Turn heat down to 225° and continue baking for approximately $3^1/_2$ hours. Gratins will be slightly firm to the touch.

Remove dishes from water bath and let cool in refrigerator overnight.

To prepare lemon cream, grate peel from remaining lemon and mince peel finely. Squeeze juice and save.

Combine half-and-half, minced lemon peel and lemon juice in large saucepan and scald. Immediately reduce to low heat.

In bowl, mix together 6 tablespoons sugar and 3 egg yolks until sugar is dissolved. Slowly add egg mixture to cream mixture, stirring constantly. Continue cooking over low heat until mixture just begins to thicken. Remove from heat. Allow to cool.

To serve, run spatula around edge of dish, separating mixture from side. Place upside down on serving plate and drizzle with lemon cream.

Makes 6 servings.

R. J. Snappers
MOCHA FLAN
Recipe of Chef John W. Skaggs

1/4 cup freshly ground coffee
1 pint heavy cream

1/4 pound dark chocolate, chopped
1/4 pound milk chocolate, chopped

8 ounces cream cheese
1/2 cup sugar
6 egg yolks

Whipped cream
Caramel topping

In saucepan, combine coffee and cream and heat just to simmer. Simmer 5 minutes, stirring occasionally.

Place both chocolates in bowl. Pour coffee and cream mixture over chocolate. Cover until chocolate is fully melted.

Using mixer cream together cream cheese, sugar and egg yolks. Add melted chocolate and cream mixture. Mix until smooth.

Pour batter into 5 or 6 individual oven-safe dishes.

Place dishes in pan(s) for water bath. Fill pan(s) halfway up with water and cover with foil.

Bake at 300° for 45 to 55 minutes.

Cool. Turn flans out onto individual plates or serve in dishes. Top with whipped cream and caramel drizzles.

Makes 5 to 6 servings.

Katzinger's
"No Truffle at All"
Chocolate Cake
Recipe of Owner Diane Warren

8	ounces semi-sweet chocolate chips
1	cup butter
6	eggs
1	cup sugar
1/8	teaspoon salt
1	teaspoon vanilla
1/2	cup flour
1/2	cup heavy cream
1 1/2	teaspoons butter
6	ounces semi-sweet chocolate chips

In microwave, melt 8 ounces chocolate chips and 1 cup butter. Stir together until smooth. Set aside.

Using mixer, thoroughly combine eggs and sugar. Add salt and vanilla. Blend in flour.

Pour melted chocolate into egg mixture and blend well.

Grease and flour 9-inch round cake pan. Pour in batter and bake at 325° for 35 to 45 minutes or until center of cake is firm but jiggles slightly when shaken. Top may be cracked slightly. Open oven door and allow cake to sit for an additional 5 minutes. Remove cake from oven and allow to cool to room temperature.

To prepare chocolate ganache, in saucepan bring cream

and butter just to boil. Remove from heat. Add chocolate chips and allow to sit for 10 to 15 minutes. Whisk until well blended, smooth and slightly thickened. Cool to room temperature before using.

Frost cake with chocolate ganache.

Makes 10 to 12 servings.

New Albany Golf Classic

Columbus Brewing Company
UPSIDE-DOWN BANANA CREAM PIE
Recipe of Chef Joe Cottage

6 1/2	tablespoons butter
1 1/4	cups graham cracker crumbs
1	cup graham cracker pieces about 1/2-inch square
2	tablespoons sugar
1/2	cup chopped pecans
1	teaspoon water
1	tablespoon sugar
1/8	teaspoon cinnamon
1	cup half-and-half
3	tablespoons cornstarch
3	egg yolks
2	teaspoons vanilla
3	tablespoons banana liqueur or extract
3	cups half-and-half
1	cup sugar
2	tablespoons butter
1/4	teaspoon salt
1 1/2	teaspoons unflavored gelatin
3/4	cup plus 2 tablespoons sugar
1/2	cup plus 1 tablespoon corn syrup
7	tablespoons butter
1	cup heavy cream
1/2	cup stout or Columbus Pale Ale

3   bananas
     Whipped cream

Melt 6 $^1/_2$ tablespoons butter. Add graham cracker crumbs and pieces. Add 2 tablespoons sugar and combine thoroughly. Set aside.

Preheat oven to 400°. Place pecans on baking sheet and bake until hot, 1 to 2 minutes. Remove from oven. Place pecans in bowl. Toss with water. Stir in 1 tablespoon sugar and cinnamon and blend until pecans are coated. Return pecans to baking sheet and bake until crisp, approximately 4 to 5 minutes. Set aside.

In small bowl, combine thoroughly 1 cup half-and-half, cornstarch, egg yolks, vanilla and banana liqueur or extract until cornstarch is fully incorporated. Set aside.

In large heavy saucepan, heat 3 cups half-and-half, 1 cup sugar, 2 tablespoons butter, salt and gelatin, stirring constantly, just to boil. Reduce heat immediately to medium. Add half-and-half/cornstarch mixture. Cook until mixture thickens and bubbles, stirring constantly. Cook 2 minutes. Remove from heat. Allow to cool to room temperature, stirring occasionally. Chill in refrigerator.

To prepare stout caramel sauce, in medium saucepan heat remaining sugar and corn syrup over medium heat until amber colored, stirring constantly, about 15 to 20 minutes. Turn off heat and slowly add butter, cream and stout, one at a time. Stir constantly until smooth. Allow to cool.

Portion graham cracker mixture into bottoms of 6 serving dishes. Top with banana custard. Slice bananas and layer on top. Top with whipped cream. Drizzle on stout-caramel sauce. Garnish with candied pecans.

Makes 6 servings.

Westerville Music and Arts Festival at Otterbein College

Notes

Notes

Index

A Taste of Columbus · Volume V
P.O. Box 215
Worthington, Ohio 43085

Please send ____ copies of
A Taste of Columbus · Vol. V to

Name _____

Address _____

City, State, Zip _____

Quantity _____ @ $16.95 each $ _____

Postage and Handling
$2.00 per book   _____

Sales Tax $0.97 per book
(Ohio residents only)   _____

Total enclosed   _____

OR

Access our website to order:
www.atasteofcolumbus.com